T0368476

The Watcher

KENNETH DAVID BRUBACHER

The Watcher

AuthorHouse™
1663 Liberty Drive
Bloomington, IN 47403
www.authorhouse.com
Phone: 1 (800) 839-8640

Illustrations by Iron Media

A Hat & Hammer Production
A Division of Brubacher Technologies Ltd.
Visit   hat&hammerproductions.com

Made in Canada

Published by AuthorHouse 10/01/2015

ISBN: 978-1-5049-5310-8 (sc)
ISBN: 978-1-5049-5311-5 (e)
ISBN: 978-1-5049-5312-2 (hc)

Library of Congress Control Number: 2015915999

Print information available on the last page.

authorHOUSE®

ALSO BY KENNETH DAVID BRUBACHER

The Poor Shoemaker

Fly

Mennonite Cobbler

There's An Angel Under My Bed

The Book of Truth and Wisdom

Leafy and Sprucy

Fire Dragon Moon

Amos and Salina Go To Town

Commotion in the ManureYard

This book is for

Micah Moses Hiller

My Grandson

A Fine Young Man

here once was a man

Who sat on hydro poles and watched

Mostly he sat on the very tops of the poles

But if there was a wire on top

Then he sat near the top but to one side

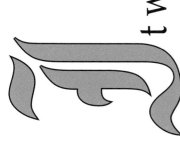

I t was not always the same pole

Sometimes it was at one end of town

Sometimes the other end

It was not a large town but not a tiny village either

You can tell how big the town was because

There were 2 Tim Hortons

This is a very good way of telling what size a town is

By how many Tim Hortons it has

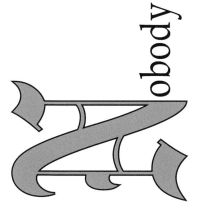obody ever saw him climb up the poles

In the morning he was just *there*   No ladder

In the evening   people tried to see him climb down

But they couldn't do it

If they turned their attention aside for even a moment

He simply *melted* or something

And was gone

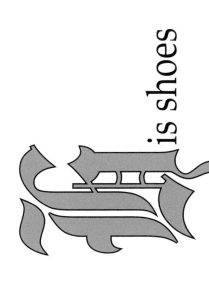 is shoes

Had no spikes to dig into the poles

There were no suction cups on his shoes either

It was a mystery

But when it was light oclock

He was always on top of a pole

When it was dark oclock   He was gone

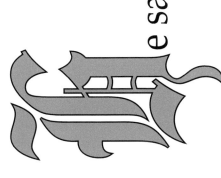e sat on something like a seat

It was hard to say

If you looked directly at him things got a bit hazy

He was clearer if you looked a bit to one side

His seat could turn around

So he could look in any direction

Nobody could figure out how the seat stayed up there

Or how it turned

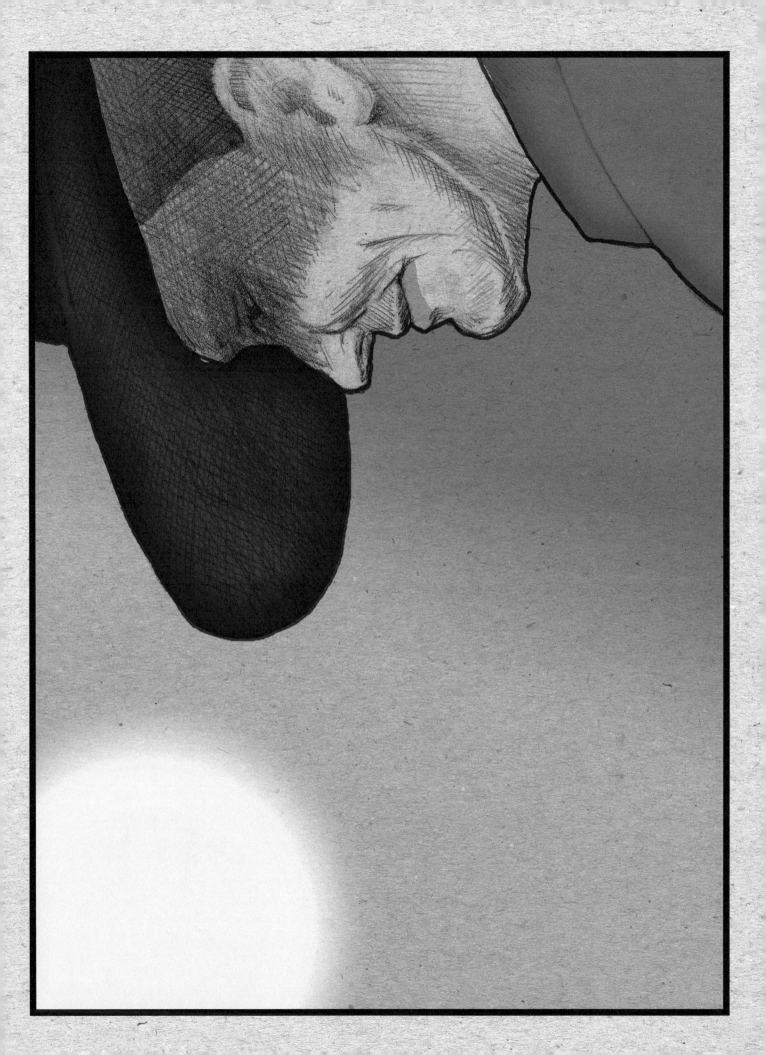

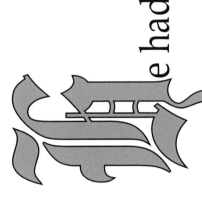He had a hat with a large brim

That shaded his face and made it hard to see

Exactly what he looked like

Several people would look at him at the same time

Some said his face looks like so and turned this way

Others would say   No   His head is turned the other way

He looks quite different to what you tell

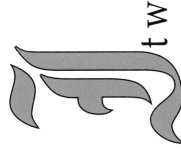It was very hard even to tell his coat color

Some said Pale Green   Others said Grey

Many were sure that it was sort of Beigey Yellow

Yet everybody agreed   he was easier to see

A bit off to one side

Looking at him dead on   he seemed to be a bit blurry

It was very strange indeed

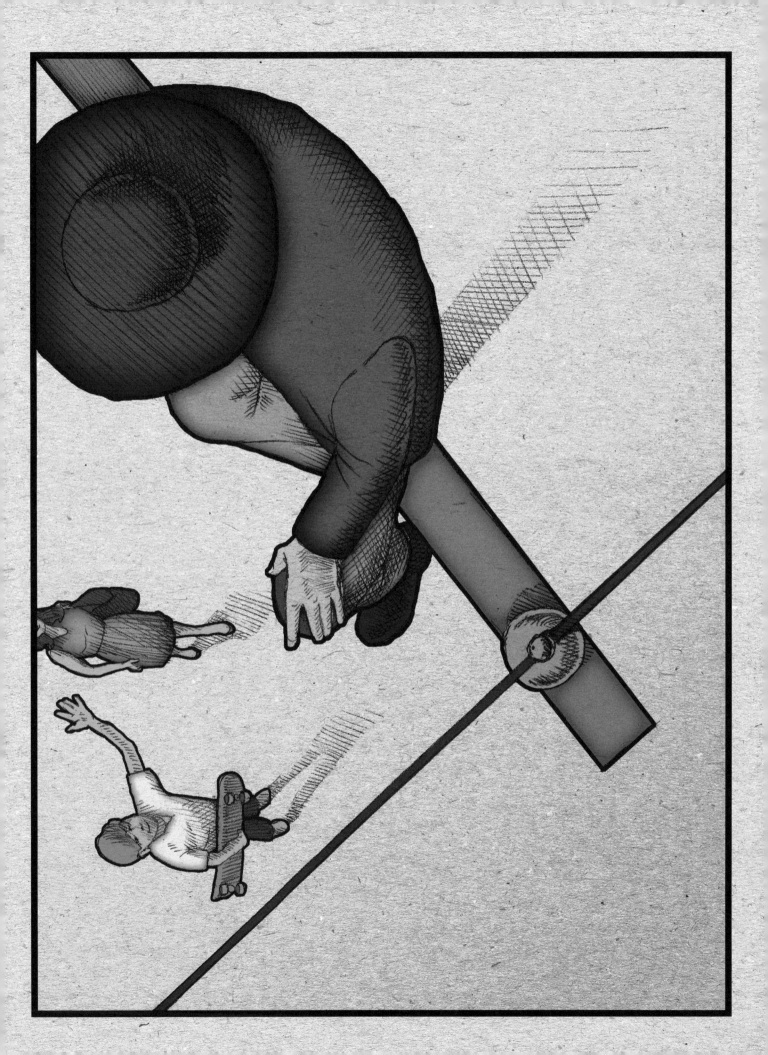

e never talked unless spoken to first

He always replied according to the time of day

A *Very Good Morning to you   Good   afternoon*

A Good Evening to you

When asked if he was hungry or thirsty

He always answered *No   But is very kind of you to ask*

He was always very polite

The weather did not seem to bother him

He wore the same coat and pants and shoes

No matter what the day was like

His hat never blew off or seemed to flutter

Even in the strongest wind

It was hard to say if he even blinked

His face never appeared to change expression

ometimes a large bird came and sat on his shoulder

People had never seen a bird exactly like that before

Oh yes   It had 2 claws and 2 legs and 2 wings

And a head on top with 2 eyes and a large beak

But it was not easy to say what color it was

Just like the mans clothes   Some people said

The bird has spots and colored places

Others said   No   The bird is plain

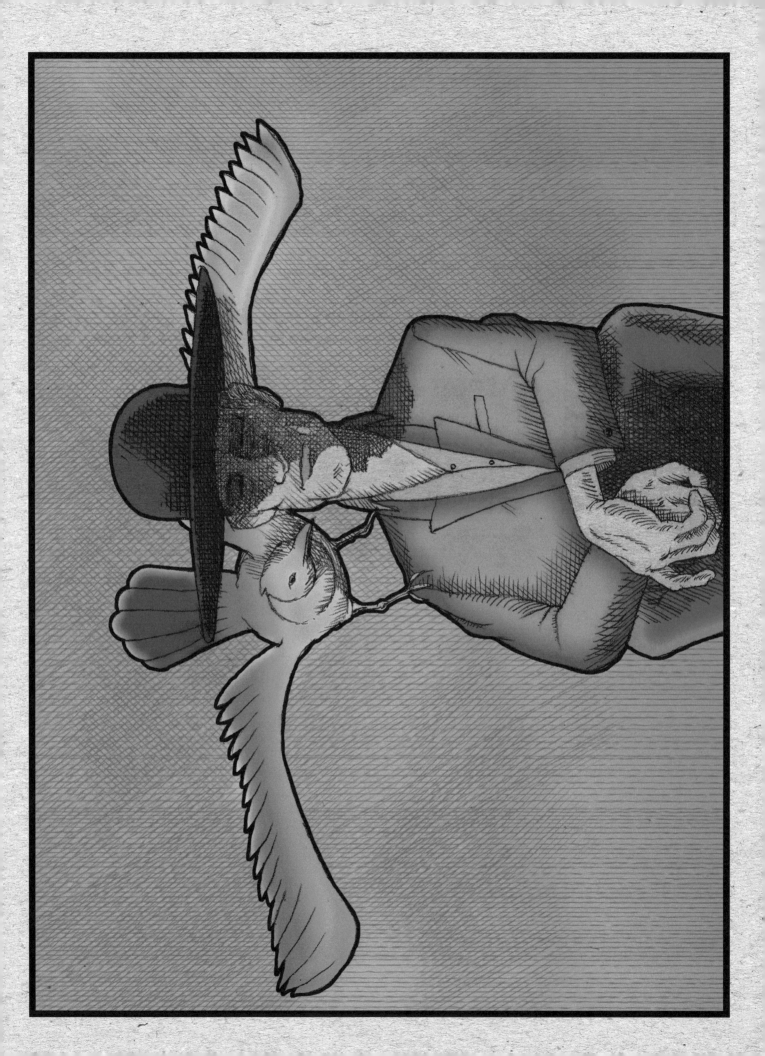

The bird *seemed* to talk to the man though his beak

Never moved   After a while the man would turn his

Face and *maybe* talk to the bird

The people thought they might have heard sounds

But could never be quite sure

When the bird flew away it was never agreed

Where the bird went   They blinked   The bird was just

Gone

People asked the Watcher what was his name

After a while he said   I am not sure anymore

It was a long time ago   And do you have relatives

He had to think about that too   I once had a brother

He was a Watcher too

He watched from a hill   People called him Fool

But he saw many things that most people do not

As all Watchers do

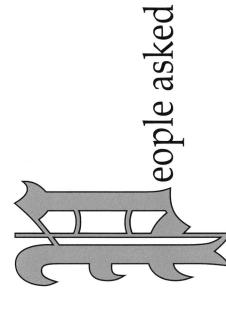eople asked

Where do you come from and why are you here

I am sent by The Keepers of The Watch

For what are you watching

I am watching for Those who will come

Then he would say nothing more about it

And carried on with his watching

eople in blue hats came   *You come down now*

They told him this with little kindness

Using a thing like what your grandmother used to

Put pickled beets into jars

The Watcher on the pole wished them *A Very Good Day*

Then a blue hat reached into his car flashing on top

And pulled out a small box on the end of a curly cord

He spoke into the box

When the watch on his wrist began to tingle

Then to buzz and hurt   He took off his watch

And put it in his pocket

But that did not help   It hurt all the more

He pulled it out of his pocket

And threw it into the back seat of the car

He looked very unhappy indeed

And rubbed his wrist and leg

oon there came other men in big yellow trucks

With lots more flashing lights   They wore yellow hats

There was with them a man in a white hat

He hollered up at the Watcher

You up there

You come down right away

Or we will go up and fetch you down

But the Watcher   Just kept on watching

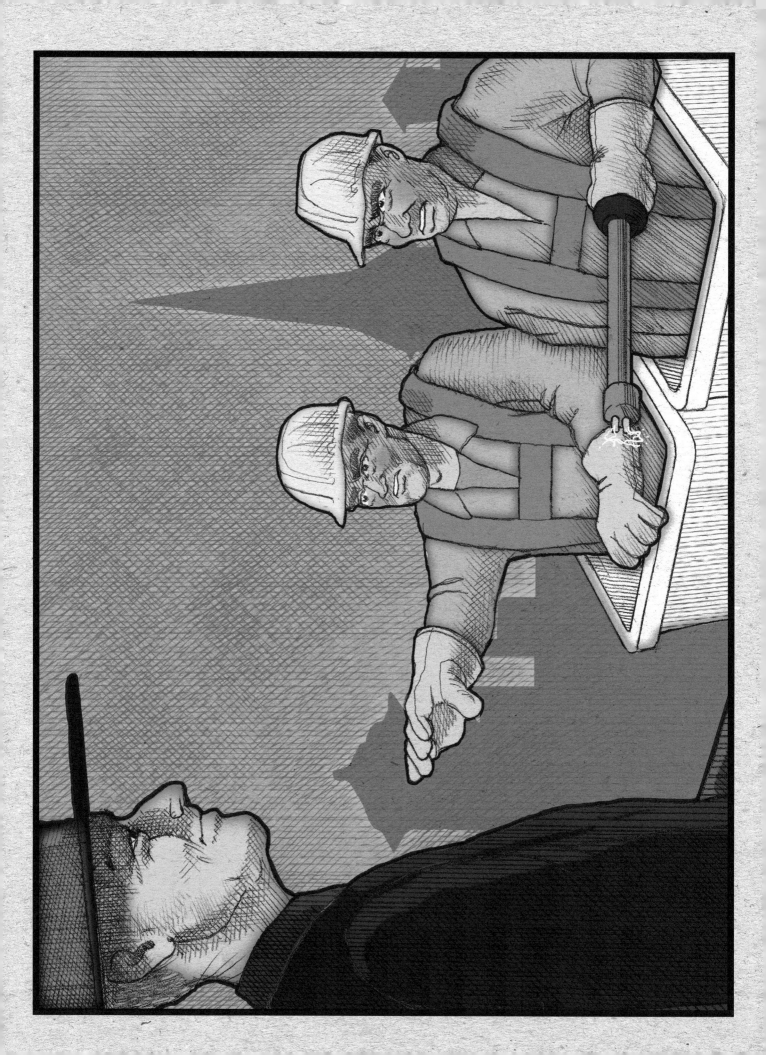

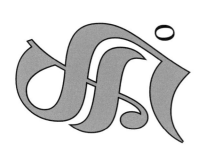

So

Two large men in yellow hats

Climbed into the buckets

On the long arm of the biggest truck

And went up to the Watcher

They were told by the man in the white hat

To take the Watcher down off the pole

hen

The watch on the hand of the man in the white hat

Started to tingle   And then to give off sparks

He yelped   And said some things that you normally

Would not learn in Sunday School

Then he quickly flung his watch into the back of his truck

He   too   rubbed his wrist

Where his watch had shocked him

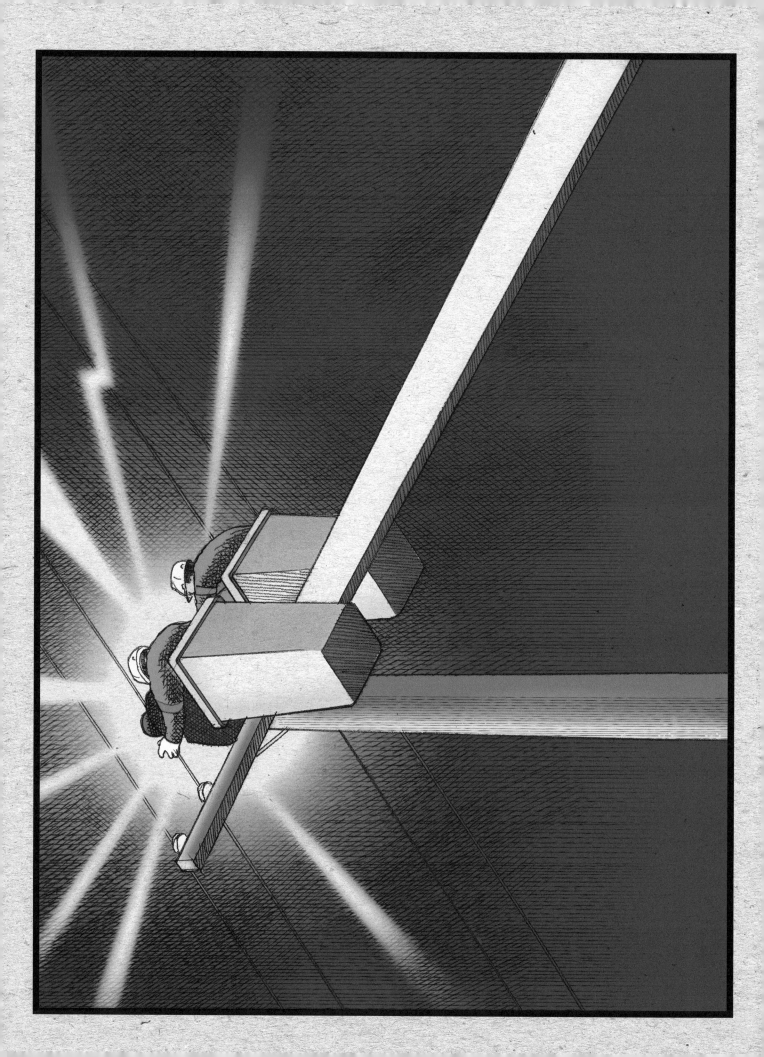

his project did not go quite to plan

To those on the ground it was hard to see exactly

What was going on up there   It was sort of fuzzy

And better seen if you looked more to one side

Those on the ground could hear crackling noises

Kind of like sparks

After a while the men in yellow hats came back down

But the Watcher was still up there

The Hats were angry and asked many hard questions

The yellow hats said it was no man up there

Maybe more like a cactus with sparks

That shocked them through their rubber protection

They normally dealt with sparking things on poles

But this time they were hurt   and confused

And had to come back down

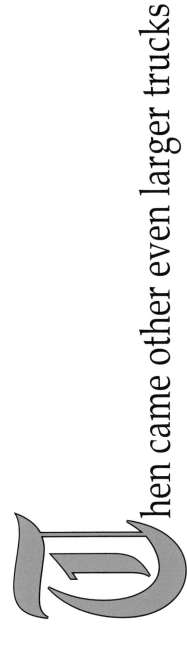
hen came other other even even larger trucks

Red trucks   With flashing lights and much loud noise

They had even even larger men in red hats

A small red truck had a man with another white hat

He spoke to the big men in the red hats

And pointed up the pole

Two large men in red hats were hoisted up

With big ladders to the top of the pole

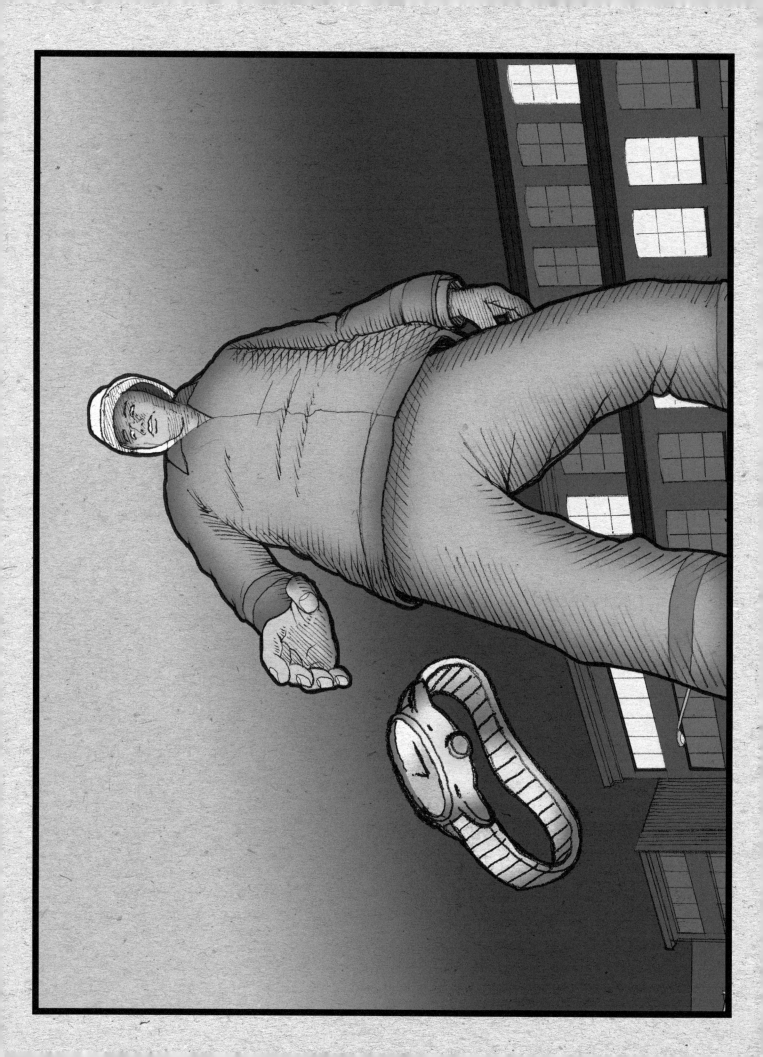

The watch on the new man with a white hat

Got warmer and warmer   And then began to get hot

So hot in fact that it would soon have burned his wrist

Had he not taken it off

He dropped it on the ground at his feet

When he tried to pick it up   It burned his fingers

So he picked it up with a stick

And threw it into the back of one of the red trucks

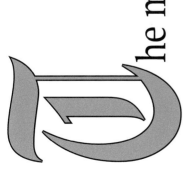

The men in red hats came down

Empty handed

They had a hard time

Looking steadily at anything for a long while

They said when they arrived at the top of the pole

It seemed that there was a creature up there

Like a very large growling throaty thing

With a lot of nasty snarling pointy teeth and claws

That seemed to come at them from all directions

o the men in the flashing cars and trucks went away

It was clear that the people liked the Watcher

And if the Men in Hats did him mischief

Then there might be problems on account of

It was soon election time   The Hats reasoned

If the yahoo on the pole fried himself   Well

What did it cost to send around the coroner

The Watcher stayed

hen the days grew shorter

Dry leaves were blown on colder winds

All that Spring and Summer the Watcher

Had always returned greetings to everybody

But when People asked him

If he could see for what he was watching

He had always said

Not yet

Uhen one day when the wind promised snow

The Watcher spoke

I have been watching to see

From which direction they shall come

And whether they will come in war or peace

My Masters now let me tell you good news

Those who shall come will not have guns

They shall drive horses   They shall wear hats of black

Nearly everybody here has become a Rushian

All rush here and rush there

And when you are done rushing over there

You come rushing right back to where you started off

You have all become Rushians

The Black Hats will teach you Quiet Enjoyment

If you let them

Listen to the music of the wind and the rain in the night

My work here finished

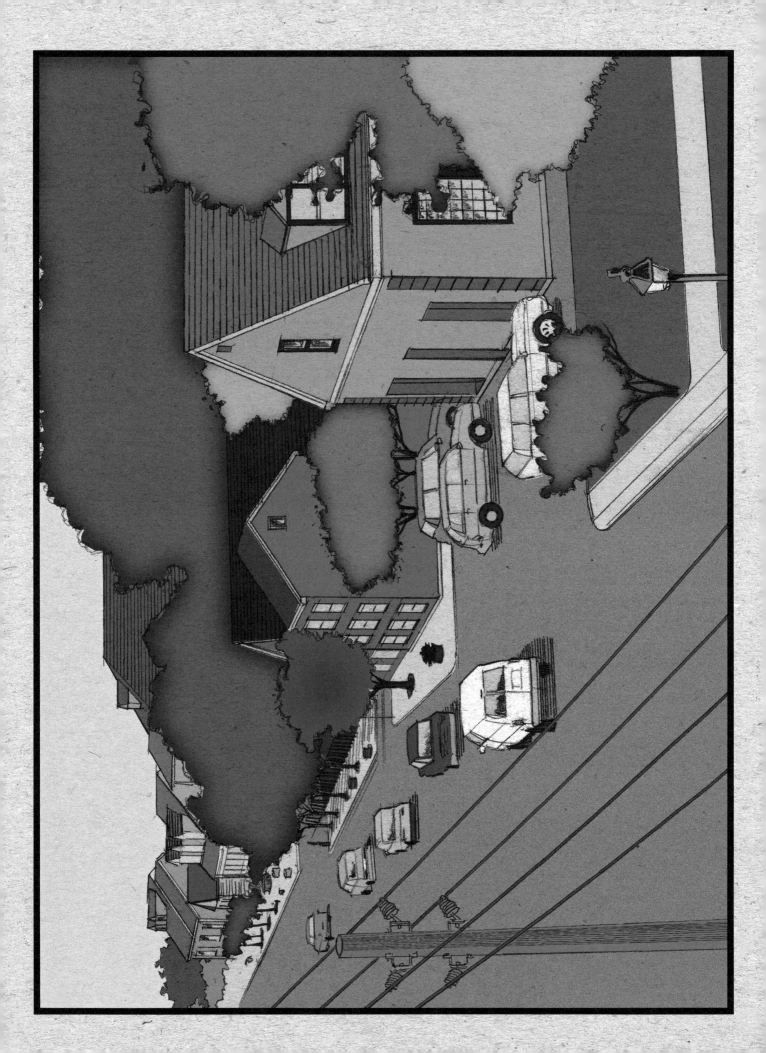

he next day the Watcher was gone

He was not on on any pole　　Or at Tim Hortons

But there was something of him still with the people

When they went and looked up to the top of a pole

Where the Watcher had been

Some could feel their watches hum a little

Or perhaps to tingle ever so slightly

Then sometimes they could see or feel

A long forgotten wonderful time or place

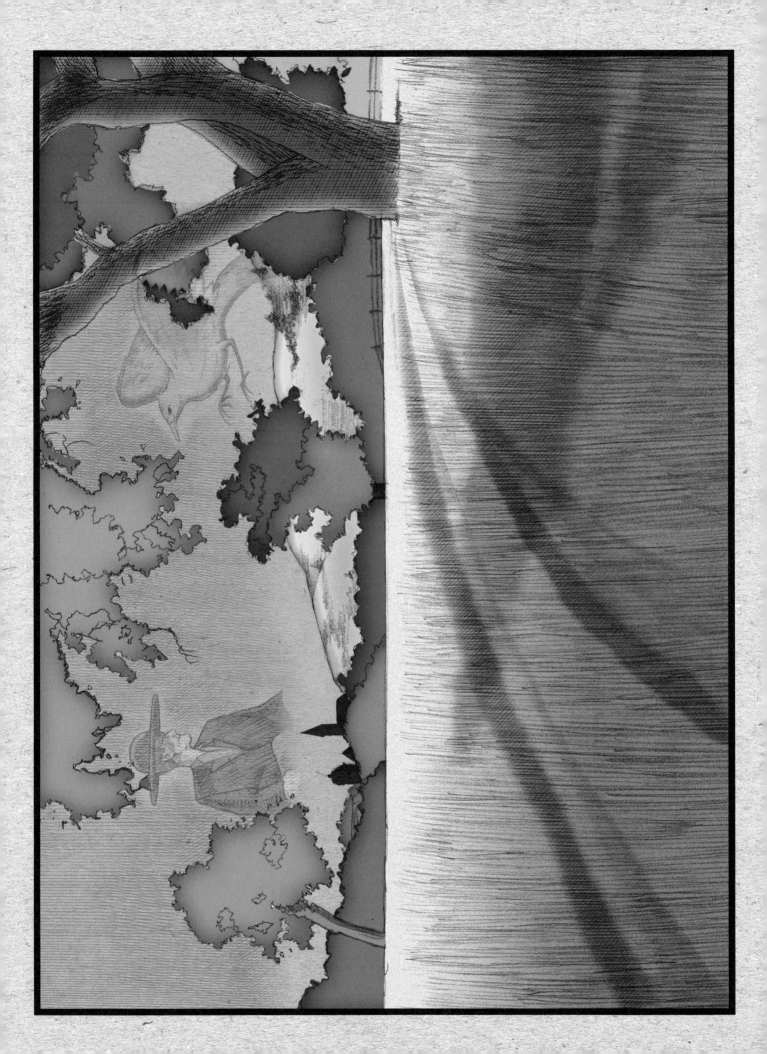

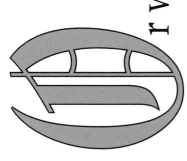r when they went to a quiet place

Where the sun rises or sets   and meditated

Out of the corner of the eye

Almost see a shimmering in a tall tree

Sense a large bird   Just over there

But when viewed more directly on was   perhaps

Gone

ABOUT THE AUTHOR

Kenneth David Brubacher was born into a large family of sort of Mennonites in Elmira, through no fault of his own. He was encouraged to make an attempt at becoming a normal human being, but with limited success. To the surprise of nearly everyone he graduated from secondary school in 1970.

From there he traveled the world extensively turning his hand to many kinds of jobs and eventually returned to Elmira having accomplished very little. He got work as a millwright but it soon was clearly evident that he was a millwrong. After being mercifully fired from that job he went trucking and almost immediately distinguished himself summa cum laude (with oak leaf cluster and Silver Star) by destroying the truck.

He got married and begat two lovely daughters which took after their mother in many wonderful ways and turned out normal. It was considered a blessing that he had no sons because there was a high degree of probability that if he had sons the little morons would turn out like their dad.

Knowing little about shoes and even less about feet he then took over his father's shop and started to make shoes by hand on April Fools' Day 1978. Very few people caught on. It was obvious that people whose feet were so bad they sought out the services of a cobbler were not very fussy. The business prospered in spite of its inherent inadequacies.

He also applied himself to many varieties of sport, establishing a universal mediocrity in their pursuit seldom seen. When his body was sufficiently trashed he took up umpiring baseball where it was observed that his training must have occurred under the tender administrations of the CNIB.

Currently he makes his home on a rented farm near Creemore and repairs a few shoes in his small shop in Collingwood. The farmhouse will soon become a gravel pit whereupon it was his intent to establish institutions where Mennonites could go to seek quiet enjoyment. This, of course, until it was pointed out to him that somebody had already done it. These establishments are known as Mennonite Farms.

The author heartily recommends that any reader who takes a notion to write and produce a book or a play, to lie down on the couch and play videos of fawns gamboling in a sun-splashed meadow full of butterflies - until the feeling goes away.

It is hoped that you enjoy the book and that its contents and presentation may provide therapeutic assistance in the remedy of your insomnia.

.

Printed in the United States
By Bookmasters